Hear Us:
An Illustrated Poem

G. Deeya

Art by: Valentina Esposito

Copyright © 2020 by G. Deeya

Written by: G. Deeya
Art by: Valentina Esposito
Layout and Edits by: Hope Boyd

All rights reserved. This book or any portion thereof may not be reproduced or used in any manner whatsoever without the express written permission of the publisher except for the use of brief quotations in a book review or scholarly journal.

First Printing: 2019
ISBN 978-1-7342370-2-3
Library of Congress Control Number: 2020922723

Grace Ekwue
752 N Main St #154
Mansfield, TX 76063-3203

G. Deeya is a Nigerian-American poet, educator, and author.
G. Deeya is Grace Ekwue's pen name.

"Dee ya" [deh-YAH] means "write it down" in Igbo (a Nigerian language). Phonetically, G. Deeya sounds like "jide ya" [gee-DEH-yah], which means "hold onto it" in Igbo.

"I wanted to write down and preserve my spoken word pieces so that they can be held and carry on."

G. Deeya was born in Nigeria, raised on the East Coast, and spent most of her life in her current state of Texas. As a former U.S. History teacher, she made time to incorporate poetry and children's books in the classroom. She has written and directed student plays and poetry showcases. When the curtains closed, her desire to preserve her writings sprung forth.

It was during this time that G. Deeya ventured into writing children's books. She carefully weaves wordplay and vivid imagery that shines through in her debut book, *Hear Us: An Illustrated Poem*.

When she is not writing, G. Deeya enjoys all the fine arts and culture that the world has to offer.

To Hope:
My first eyes and ears

Christianity is the only major religion in which you can celebrate the holidays without ever mentioning the deity. You can simply change the focus.

With Christmas, focus on Santa or good will toward men.
With Easter, focus on the Easter bunny or gift baskets and family photos.

If only we could find the time to reflect about God's sacrifice and love. Then, we would realize that these miraculous events hold more than enough wonder in and of themselves.

JESUS...

From the womb,
You could still hear us...

A growing babe,
yet fully God,

Son of Man
sent down to save
helpless souls
who didn't know
they needed

...A SAVIOR.

You saved Your
glory for later.

Knowing You'll be rejected,
stepping down from Your throne,

You accepted the shift from
right hand of God

to

left to the masses

who

denied You were
the coming Messiah.

You weren't like us...

In wisdom and stature,
You grew.

In favor with God and Man,
You knew

Your Father's business.

More than a
carpenter's apprentice,
You were Your Father's witness.

Preparing to be our final sacrifice,

learning the Law of Moses,
so descendants of Abraham

could pull You
out of the thicket,

as the ram
chosen to cover our sin...

Forgive us.

Buried under "early bird specials", Black Friday deals,

light fights for the best winter wonderlands...

We stand,
in long queues,
so kids can get
pics and wishes
granted by Claus.

Granted, it's cute.

But couldn't it cause confusion
and dilute the real cause?
The true... clause?

The real
subject and verb
of Christmas?

God's Son,
dressed in humility,
stepped into humanity,
so that He could relate.

And in the end...

reinstate us
to a Father
who's been trying to restore
sons and daughters
to an Eden-like connection

since The Fall.

That's all...
That's all He wants.

Your time,
your love,
is that too much?

Who sacrificed more?
God or Us?

God With Us...
Emmanuel,
come, dwell near us...

see that we need to
take You

out of the manger,
off the cross,
out of the tomb.

You've been out of the womb
over 2,000 years,

waiting for us
to make the connection...

between our brokenness
and the Hope of Salvation.

Find Christ This Season...

I remember reading Chick tracts after Sunday school in Maryland. They were cartoon booklets that shared the Gospel message by the last few pages.

I'm going to use that approach to help those who need to find Christ this season.

No matter what you've done or will do, God loves you; and He wants to spend eternity with you. He doesn't force us to love Him back. He allows us to choose how we want to live our life and where we'll spend it after our time on earth is over.

Becoming a Christian is simply the process of realizing who Jesus is and why you need Him in your life.

It is about realizing that everyone is a sinner, and sin separates us from God.

It is about believing Jesus is God's son who died and rose for us so that when we die, we can go to heaven to be with God. Without God, our lives are empty. Jesus fills the void and gives life meaning, purpose, and direction.

Once you realize these things and make the decision to turn your life around and allow Jesus is guide your life, you are a Christian.

The Bible spells it out in greater detail. It says:

Doing good things cannot save you.

"For it is by grace you have been saved, through faith; and this is not from yourselves, it is the gift of God — not by works, so that no one can boast." (Ephesians 2:8-9)

There is only one way to Heaven.

"Jesus answered, 'I am the way and the truth and the life. No one comes to the Father except through me.'" (John 14:6)

THE WAY TO HEAVEN IS THROUGH JESUS CHRIST, GOD'S ONLY SON. HERE'S HOW YOU CAN BECOME A CHRISTIAN:

1. Admit you are a sinner and have made mistakes.
- "... For all have sinned and fall short of the glory of God." (Romans 3:23)
- "As it is written, 'There is none righteous, not even one.'" (Romans 3:10)

2. Be willing to turn away from sin (repent).
- "Repent, then, and turn to God, so that your sins may be wiped out..." (Acts 3:19)
- "In the same way, I tell you, there is rejoicing in the presence of the angels of God over one sinner who repents." (Luke 15:10)

3. Believe that Jesus Christ died for you, was buried, and rose from the dead.
- "For God so loved the world that he gave his one and only Son, that whoever believes in him shall not perish but have eternal life." (John 3:16)
- "But God demonstrates his own love for us in this: While we were still sinners, Christ died for us." (Romans 5:8)
- "If you declare with your mouth, 'Jesus is Lord,' and believe in your heart that God raised him from the dead, you will be saved." (Romans 10:9)

4. Through prayer, invite Jesus into your life to become your personal Savior.

"... For everyone who calls on the name of the Lord will be saved." (Romans 10:13)

Here's what you can pray: "Dear God, I know I am a sinner and need forgiveness. I believe that Jesus Christ died for my sins and rose from the dead. I am willing to turn from sin. Jesus, come into my heart. I trust and follow you as my Lord and Savior. Help me to live for you from now on. In Jesus' name, amen."

Congratulations! You've just accepted Jesus Christ as your personal Savior and secured your spot in Heaven. Get connected with a Bible-teaching church to continue growing as a Christian.

"Therefore, if anyone is in Christ, the new creation has come: The old has gone, the new is here!" (2 Corinthians 5:17)

Also By G. Deeya:

"More Than Extra"

www.ingramcontent.com/pod-product-compliance
Lightning Source LLC
Chambersburg PA
CBHW041820040426
42452CB00004B/157